CONTENTS

Chapter 1 1
Chapter 2 6
Chapter 3 10
Chapter 4 15
Chapter 5 20
Chapter 6 28
Chapter 7 33
Chapter 8 40
Chapter 9 46
Chapter 10 50
Chapter 11 55

The Road to Somewhere

Tana Reiff

A Pacemaker® *WorkTales* Book

FEARON/JANUS
Belmont, California

Simon & Schuster Supplementary Education Group

WorkTales

A Robot Instead
The Easy Way
Change Order
Fighting Words
The Rip-Offs
The Right Type
The Saw that Talked
Handle with Care
The Road to Somewhere
Help When Needed

Cover illustration: Terry Hoff
Interior illustration: James Balkovek

ISBN 0-8224-7154-X
Library of Congress Catalog Card Number: 91-70782
Printed in the United States of America
1. 9 8 7 6 5 4 3 2

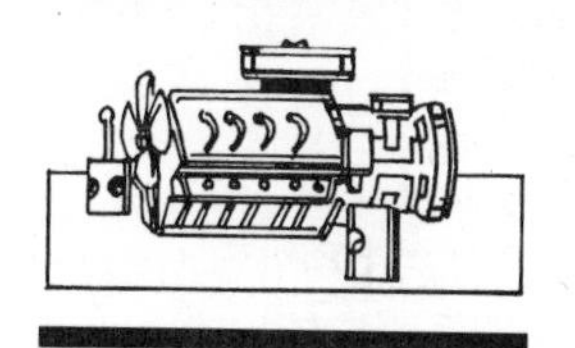

CHAPTER 1

"I must *WHAT*?"
said Buck Harding
in a very loud voice.

"You must take
a truck driver's test,"
Garth Skinner said again.

"I already have a license,"
said Buck.

"This is a *new* license,"
said Garth.

"I've been driving
a milk tank truck
for 20 years,"
said Buck.
"My old company
goes out of business.
I come here to find a job

with my old buddy's company.
Now all of a sudden
Uncle Sam says
I have to take a test
to do what I've done
for 20 years.
Does someone think
I don't know what I'm doing
after all this time?"

"No one is saying that,"
said Garth.
"You and everyone else
are in the same boat.
And you're not the only one
who's hot about this.
I'll tell you what.
We're going to hold a class
here at Skinner's Dairy.
It's four hours
on four Friday afternoons.
It starts next week.
It won't cost you
anything but your time.
You'll learn what you need

for the test.
If you don't pass
the first time,
you get two more tries."

"I have a great record,"
said Buck.
"I've never hurt a fly.
Doesn't that mean something?"

"It means you won't need
to take the road test,"
said Garth.
"But you still need to take
three parts of the written test.
It's the law, buddy.
You must get the new license
or you're off the road."

Buck rolled his eyes.
He didn't say anything.
He was thinking
that he could never handle
the book work.
He had dropped out of school

as soon as he turned 16.
In the years since then,
he had learned a lot
about tank trucks.
But go back to school?
Take a test, too?
No way.

"See you later,"
Buck told Garth.
"I'm heading home."

"I want to hire you, buddy,"
Garth called after Buck.
"Pass the test
and I'll take you on.
I can't do anything for you
without that license.
You can do it."

"Sure, I can,"
said Buck.
"Make it out the door—
that's about all I can do,"
he whispered to himself.

Thinking It Over

1. Suppose you had worked
   at a job
   for many years.
   How would you feel
   if you then had
   to pass a test?

2. Why does the government
   make people in some jobs
   have a license
   to do their work?

3. Do you think it is fair
   to make people
   pass a test
   for certain jobs?

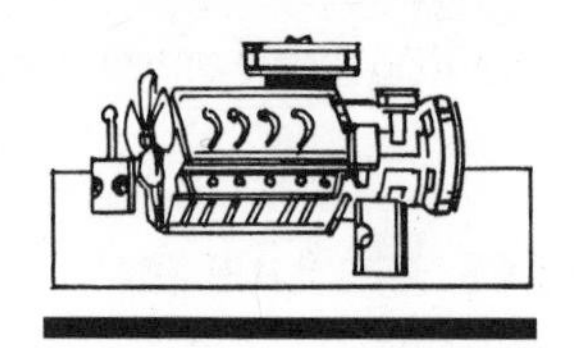

CHAPTER 2

"There's only one thing
you can do,"
said Buck's wife Lorna
when he told her.
"You go to the class.
You get yourself ready
for the test.
Then you do your best."

"But Lorna,"
Buck started.
"Pencils and books
are not my thing.
I would hate
every minute
of that class."

"How do you know?"
asked Lorna.
"You haven't been there yet."

"And if I can help it,
I *won't* be there, either,"
said Buck.
"I don't even read that good."

"Hand me that can,"
said Lorna,
pointing to the kitchen sink.

Buck picked up
the can of fruit
Lorna had left beside the sink.

"What does it say
on this can?"
Lorna asked.

"It says *Mixed Fruit,*"
said Buck.

"You're right,"
said Lorna.

"Babe, a truck license test
is a far cry

from a can of fruit,"
said Buck.

"Listen to me,"
said Lorna.
"You're going to sign up
for that class.
You're going to study
your shirt off.
And I'm going to help you.
You hear me?"

"I hear you, Babe,"
said Buck.
"What else can I do?
I'm stuck between a rock
and a hard place.
I either do this
or I'll have to sell hot dogs
on the street
and wear a silly hat."

"So what if you do?"
said Lorna.
"I would still love you."

Thinking It Over

1. What does it mean to be
   "between a rock
   and a hard place"?
   Have you ever been
   in such a place?

2. How important is it
   to have help
   when you have to face
   something you're afraid of?

3. Do you think
   Buck is a weak person?
   Why or why not?

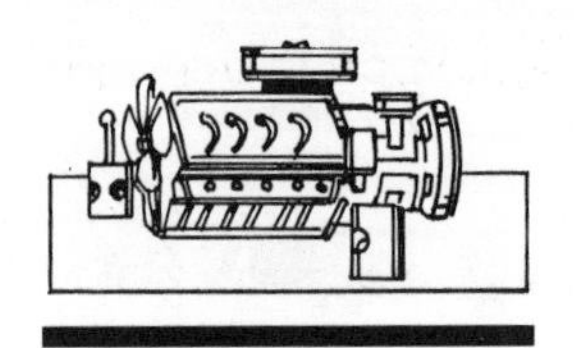

CHAPTER 3

The next day
Buck went back to Skinner's.
He signed up
for the drivers' class.
There he met
the teacher, Candy Barr.

"Is that your real name—
Candy Barr?"
Buck asked her.

"It really is,"
laughed Candy.
"I guess my parents
were trying to be funny.
Is that your real name—
Buck Harding?"

"My real name
is Miles Harding,"

said Buck.
"What would you think
of a truck driver named Miles?
I guess when it comes
to funny names,
I have no room to talk."

Candy and Buck
both laughed.
Then she told Buck
about the tests
he would have to take.
First there would be
a written test of facts.
All the drivers
had to take that one.
Buck would also have to take
a test only for drivers
of tank trucks.
And he would have to take
another test on air brakes.
Buck didn't have to take
the road test
because he had
a clean record.

"When you pass
all the tests
you need to take,
you'll get your CDL,"
Candy went on.
"CDL stands for
Commercial Driver's License."

"What are the tests like?"
Buck wanted to know.

"I won't kid you,"
said Candy.
"They're not easy.
You'll need to know
a great many facts.
I know you've been driving
a long time.
However, I do think
you'll pick up
some new things."

"I'd rather drop
the whole thing!"
Buck said.

"Is that what
you really want to do?"
Candy asked him.

"I just want
to drive again,"
said Buck.
"But I have to tell you.
I feel like a big dope."

"Guess what?"
said Candy.
"You're not the first person
to tell me that.
See you in class
Friday afternoon."

Thinking It Over

1. How has Buck taken
   the first step?
   Why is the first step
   often the hardest to take?

2. How is Candy
   trying to make Buck
   feel better about things?

3. Do you like it
   when a teacher
   acts like a friend?
   Why or why not?

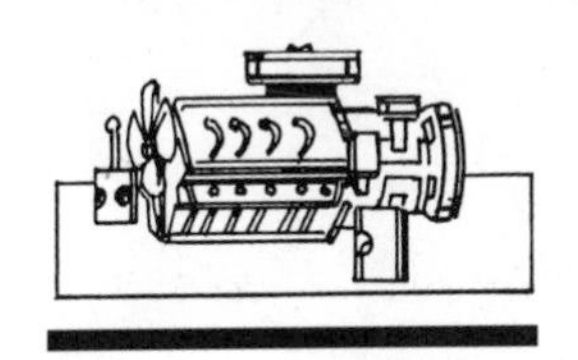

CHAPTER 4

Friday took its time
getting there.
All week,
Buck couldn't get his mind
off the driver's test.

By lunch time Friday,
it had become a big worry.
He didn't see how
he could show up
for the class.
Still, Buck drove his car
over to Skinner's Dairy.
The whole way,
he was thinking
about other driver's tests
he had taken.
He had worked hard
to drive a car and a truck.
If he could pass those tests,
maybe he could pass one more.

He ate lunch
in Skinner's lunch room.
Then he walked up and down
the long hall
by the classroom.
He lit up
one smoke after another.
Just then,
Garth Skinner came by.

"Isn't it time
for the drivers' class
to begin?"
asked Garth.

"Looks that way,"
said Buck.

"Why don't you go in?"
asked Garth.

"Not feeling so good,"
said Buck.
"Maybe it's something
I ate for lunch."

"I saw you
in the lunch room,"
said Garth.
"Everybody ate the same.
No one else is sick."

"It really hurts more
in my head,"
said Buck.
"I probably should
just go home
and lie down."

"It's in your head, all right,"
said Garth.
"Look, Buck.
It's up to you.
You can go to the class.
Or you don't have to.
You can try
to take the test
without the class.
Or you can just give up
right this minute.
What's it going to be?"

Buck stuffed
the pack of smokes
back into his pocket.
"I guess it's back to school,"
he said.
With that, he stepped
into the classroom.

Thinking It Over

1. What is something new
   you were afraid
   to get started on?
   Why were you afraid?

2. When has someone
   helped to talk you
   into doing something?

3. Have you ever
   made up excuses
   to try to get
   out of something?

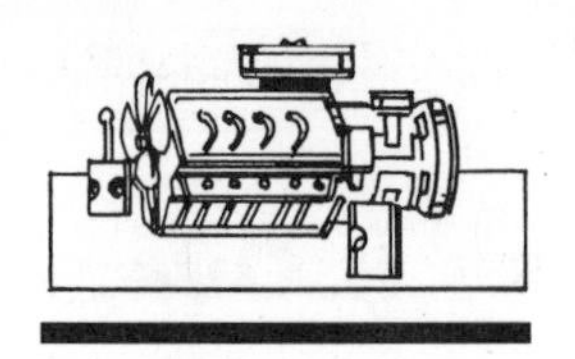

CHAPTER 5

Inside the classroom
were 12 other drivers—
ten men and two women.
They had come
from different companies.
They drove different kinds
of trucks and buses.
No one looked very happy
to be there.

Candy stood by a table
along the side.
She was passing out
cups of coffee.
"Have a donut,"
she called to Buck.
He went over and reached
for a sugar donut.
His hand shook a little
as he took a cup of coffee.

Some of the people
were crowded around the tables
along the other side.
Buck walked over
to see what was going on.
Oh, no, he said to himself.
It was a row of computers.
That's all I need,
Buck was thinking.
It's bad enough I'm here at all.
Now they throw in
computers, too.
He wanted to back
out the door.
But Candy broke in
on his plan.

"Do the computers
look interesting to you?"
she asked Buck.

"Not really,"
said Buck.
"I've never touched
a computer in my life."

"Do you have a VCR at home?"
Candy asked.
"When you set your VCR
to tape a show,
you're using a computer.
But these teaching computers
are much more fun than a VCR.
They ask you questions.
Then they tell you
if you gave the right answer."

Candy asked everyone
to sit down.
She passed out some papers.
"First, let's answer
a few simple questions,"
she said.
She read each question.
It was easy
for Buck to follow along.

"Number one,"
Candy began.
"How do you feel
about taking the driver's test?

Number two.
How do your family members
feel about your taking the test?"

They talked about the questions.
Buck was happy to say
that Lorna was behind him.
He was sure
that would be important.

Then Candy held up
a little book.
"This is the CDL manual,"
she began.
She told the class
how the computer
would help them get ready
for the CDL test.
There were six computers
in the room.
"We'll pair you up,"
Candy explained.

Buck counted heads again.
Yes, there were 13 people.

If Candy put two people
on each computer,
there would still be
one too many persons here.
I must be the one too many,
Buck said to himself.

But Candy had other ideas.
The class would spend
part of the time
at the big tables in the center.
There, they would write
in lesson books.
The rest of the time
they would work
on the computers.

Candy broke the class
into little teams.
Each team
had two or three people.
People on the same team
drove the same kind of truck.
They would study together.
She put Buck

with another tank truck driver.
His name was Simms.

Buck was afraid
Simms would make fun of him.
But Simms was a nice guy.
He was a good reader.
He helped Buck
as the two of them
worked on the first lesson.

After class,
Candy stopped Buck
on his way out the door.
"How's it going?"
she asked.

"So far, so good,"
said Buck.
He looked a lot better
than when he came in.

"I was glad to hear
your wife is behind you on this,"
said Candy.

"Lorna's behind me, all right,"
said Buck.
"By the time
I get done with this,
she'll be able
to pass the test, too.
Just you wait."

"Take the first book home,"
said Candy.
"Lorna can help you study."

Buck wasn't wild
about being Lorna's student.
But he felt he needed
all the help he could get.

He showed Lorna the book
when he got home.
She really wanted to help.
The two of them
went right to work
that very night.

Thinking It Over

1. If you were working
   on something,
   how much help
   would you want
   from your family or friends?

2. When you were afraid
   to start something new,
   how did things work out?

3. Do you work better alone
   or on a team?

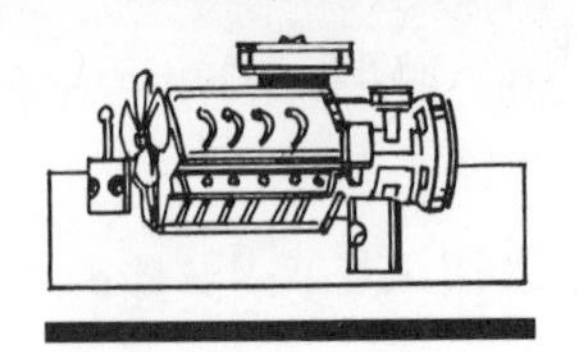

CHAPTER 6

For the next three Fridays
Buck went to the CDL class.
It wasn't easy for him.
But there was a lot to like.
Candy was a great teacher.
Buck got to know Simms.
He was a good guy.
The whole class
became friends.
And Buck had to admit
he was learning things.

The best part
was working on the computer.
It was like playing a game.
Buck and all the others
came to enjoy it a lot.

Candy showed him
which parts of the CDL books

he should work on.
She also gave Buck a video
to watch at home.

Buck loved
to watch TV.
He couldn't wait
to get home
and watch the video.

As soon as he got home,
he popped the tape
into the VCR.
Before long,
the two kids,
Dawn and Dirk,
came in to watch with him.

Then Lorna
got home from work.
She carried a bag of food
in each arm.
"What are you all
so tuned into?"
she asked them.

"Dad got us
a new video,"
said Dirk.

Lorna looked over
at the TV.
She saw words
on the screen.
They were questions
about a truck's engine.
She saw pictures
of the insides
of a truck's air brakes.
"Dad brought home
a new video for the kids, huh?"
she laughed.
"I'll just put down these bags.
Then I'll watch with you."

The four of them
watched the whole tape.

"It sure beats
some of the shows
you kids watch,"

laughed Lorna.
"Did you learn anything?"
she asked as she turned to Buck.

Before Buck could answer,
Dawn broke in.
"Let's watch it again!"
she screamed.

"Sure," said Buck.
"Candy said I should watch it
more than one time."
He pushed a button
to start the tape over.
Then they all watched it
one more time.

Thinking It Over

1. Have you ever been afraid
   of something
   and then learned to enjoy it?

2. What have you ever learned
   from a video?

3. Why can a video
   be a good way
   for some people to learn?

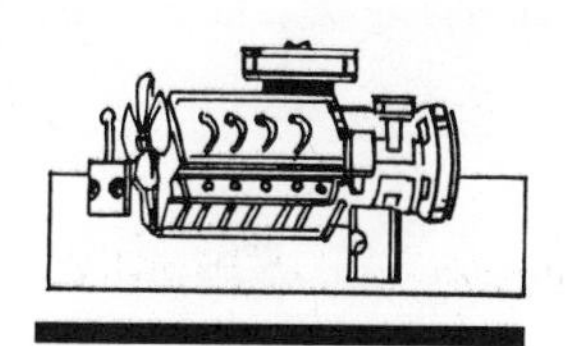

CHAPTER 7

The next morning,
Lorna and Buck
sat down together.
Lorna said it was time
to study for the tank truck test.

"I'll ask you questions,"
Lorna began.
"You give me the answers.
Ready?
Why should you
go slow on curves?"

"Because a tank truck
is top-heavy,"
said Buck.
"It's easy to roll over."

"Right," said Lorna.
"Next question.
What is a smooth bore tank?"

"That's easy,"
said Buck.
"It has no baffles
to divide up the inside
of the tank.
It's for liquid food cargo.
A tank with baffles
can't be kept
clean enough for food."

"Why is a smooth bore truck
hard to drive?"
asked Lorna.

"Because the cargo
moves around so much,"
said Buck.
"It makes a strong
forward-and-back surge."

"You know all this,"
said Lorna.
"Let's go look at a truck!"

"I know
what a truck looks like,"
said Buck.

"Of course you do,"
said Lorna.
"I mean,
let's go study
how to check over a truck."

So Buck and Lorna
drove down to Skinner's.
Garth gave them
the keys to a milk truck.
They parked
next to a row
of milk tank trucks.
Lorna got out the CDL book.

"Say this is your truck,"
said Lorna.
"We'll go over
the seven pre-trip steps."

First Buck looked over
the whole truck.
Lorna crawled under the truck.
"Look here," she said.
"Here's a fresh oil leak."

"Can't go out like that,"
said Buck.
The second step
was to check the engine.
Buck checked the oil
and other fluids.
He checked the belts.

Third, Buck climbed
into the cab.
He started the engine.
He checked all the controls.
He checked the mirrors.
He looked at everything.
Fourth, he turned off the engine.
He checked the lights
from inside the cab.
"Are the low beams on?"
Buck called to Lorna.

"Get out and look yourself,"
she said.
"OK, you're done.
Now let's do
the full walk-around."

She and Buck
walked all the way
around the truck.
They checked windows.
They checked wheels.
They checked brakes.
They checked tires.
You name it,
they checked it.

Number six
was to check the lights
all around the truck.

Finally, it was time
for number seven.
Buck started the engine again.
He tested the brakes.
Then he made sure

all the right papers
were in the cab.

"We're done,"
said Lorna.
"Fix that oil leak
and you're road-ready.
Where do you want to go?"

"How about some place
with a big, white beach?"
said Buck.

"Let's go!"
said Lorna.
But they didn't drive away
in the truck.
Instead, they locked it up.
They dropped off the keys
in Garth's office.
They got back into their car
and drove home
for dinner with the kids
and a long lesson
on air brakes.

Thinking It Over

1. Do you think
   that getting ready
   for the CDL test
   is as bad as Buck
   believed it would be?

2. Why is it important
   to know a lot
   about the job you do?

3. What can you do
   to make a hard job more fun?

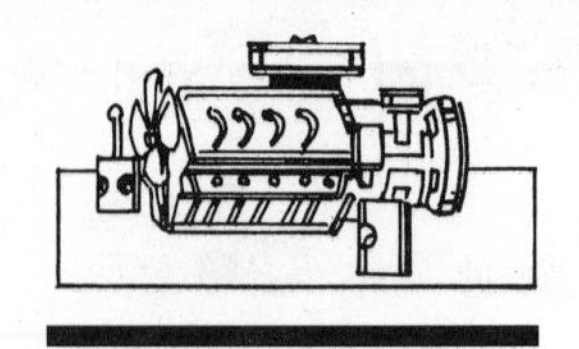

CHAPTER 8

For the first few weeks,
Buck was glad
for Lorna's help.
As much help as he got
from the CDL class,
he needed more.
Even when the class was over,
Lorna was there
to be his second teacher.
One day Lorna said,
"We're going out
to look at air brakes."

Maybe Buck
wasn't in the mood
to hear that.
Maybe it was the way
Lorna said it.
Whatever the reason,
Buck didn't take it well.

"What do you mean,
'We're going out
to look at air brakes'?"
he barked.
"I'm watching a game
and I don't feel like going.
And who are you
to tell me what to do?"

"Gee, Buck, I'm sorry,"
said Lorna.
"I was only trying to help."

"Well, you've helped enough,"
said Buck.

"I just want you
to pass the test,"
said Lorna.
She began to cry.

"It's like I told Candy,"
Buck said.
"I said by the time
I get done with this,

Lorna will be able
to pass the test, too.
So why don't you
just go and take the test for me?"

"Don't be silly,"
said Lorna.
"You know I can't do that."

"Well, you could pass
if you did take the test,"
said Buck.

"Maybe I could,"
said Lorna.
"So what?"

"Because I have some news,"
said Buck.
"I already took the first test.
I was afraid I wouldn't pass.
So I didn't tell you or anyone.
That's where I was last Saturday
when I said I was shopping
for new tools.

And guess what?
I was right.
I didn't pass.
Simms made it but I didn't."

Lorna walked over
to put her arm around Buck.
"I'm sorry, honey,"
she said.

"Forget it,"
said Buck,
as he pushed her away.
"I have to face facts.
After 20 years on the road,
I'm *off* the road."

"Wait one little minute,"
said Lorna.
"You told me you get
three shots at the test.
So you have two more to go."

"I'll only mess up again,"
said Buck.

"I'll help you study more,"
said Lorna.

"I'm sick of being
your student," said Buck.
"You just take over
the whole show.
You horn in on everything.
You seem to forget
who's the man around here."

"Maybe I do push a little,"
said Lorna.
"But that has nothing to do
with being a man or a woman.
Give it a rest, Buck.
You can pass that test.
And I can help you."

"I said forget it,"
said Buck.
"Tomorrow I'll start
to look for a job.
And it won't be
behind any wheel."

Thinking It Over

1. How would you feel
   if you took an important test
   and didn't pass?

2. Do you think
   Buck is right
   to look for
   a different kind of job?

3. How can Lorna help Buck
   if he doesn't want her help?

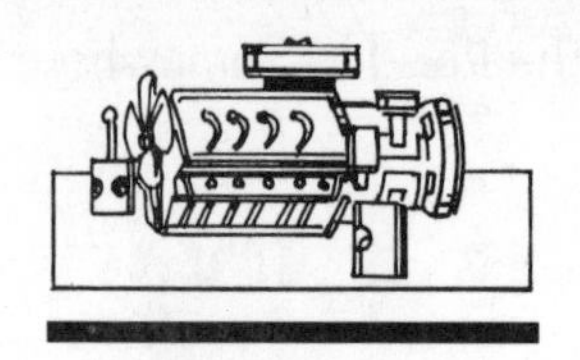

CHAPTER 9

Lorna didn't push.
She didn't even talk
about the CDL test.
She waited for Buck
to change his mind
about the test.

On Friday afternoon,
Buck came home
from his job hunt.
"I think I found a job,"
he told Lorna.
"I can start on Monday."

"What's the job?"
Lorna wanted to know.

"I'll be working
on the loading dock
at Skinner's Dairy,"

said Buck.
"Garth felt sorry for me.
He said he'd take me on."

"You on the loading dock?"
Lorna said.
"Do you think
you would like that?
That's real hard work."

"So is driving a milk truck,"
said Buck.
"I can handle it."

"OK, OK,"
said Lorna.
"But why do you say
'I *think* I found a job'?"

"Because there's a catch,"
said Buck.
"Garth said I could work for him
only if I take the CDL test again.
I said I would.
But maybe I lied."

"I won't put in my two cents,"
said Lorna.
"Do what you want."

"I will, Babe,"
Buck said.
"You can count on that.
Now I have to get ready
for my new job.
Where are those weights
I used to lift?"

"They're on the floor
behind your work clothes,"
Lorna told him.
"But don't try too much at first.
You haven't lifted weights
since high school."

"Like I said,
don't tell me what to do,"
Buck shot back.
"I know what I can do.
And I know what I can't do.
So mind your own business."

Thinking It Over

1. Think of something
   you have done
   that had a "catch."
   Was the catch worth it?

2. When do you know
   that something is
   none of your business?

3. What makes a job
   right for a person?

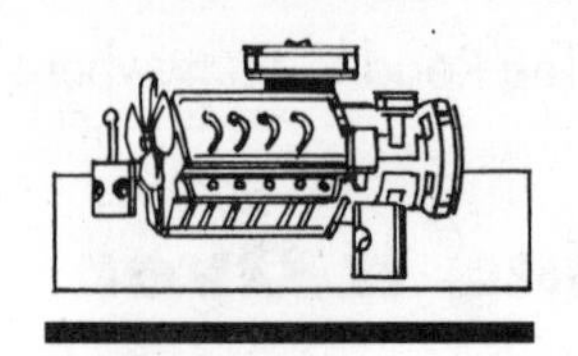

CHAPTER 10

Buck lifted weights
all morning Saturday.
After lunch,
he went at it again.
Lorna heard him
make the noises people make
when they lift something heavy.
She knew he must be in pain.

Sunday morning
she saw how right she was.
She woke up before Buck.
She went to the kitchen
to start breakfast.
Just as she reached
for the egg pan,
she heard a loud
"HELP ME!"
It was Buck.
He couldn't get out of bed.

"You were right, Babe,"
he cried.
"I should have listened to you.
I pushed it too hard yesterday.
I'm not 17 years old.
What in the world
was I trying to do?"

Lorna helped him
sit up in bed.
She rubbed his neck.
Then she helped him
lie down on his stomach.
She rubbed his back.
She rubbed his arms.
She rubbed his legs.

At last, Buck was ready
to try to get out of bed.
He tried to swing
one leg at a time
down to the floor.
"That hurts,"
he said about ten times.
Finally, he was on his feet.

"I have to call Garth,"
he said.

"Are you going to tell him
you can't make it tomorrow?"
Lorna asked.

"I have to tell him
I can't make it *ever,*"
said Buck.
"No way, no how
do I want to work
on the loading dock.
It'll kill me before my time."

They ate breakfast
with the kids.
Then Dawn and Dirk
ran off to play.

"What do you want to do today?"
Lorna asked Buck.

"Read the funnies
and go back to bed,"

said Buck.
"Then I'd like to do something."

"What's that?"
said Lorna.

"Let's go down to Skinner's
and look at air brakes,"
said Buck.
"And then let's come home
and hit the books
like never before.
What do you say?
Are you with me?"

Lorna smiled.
"I'm with you,"
she said.
"But there's one catch.
I can't push you."

"Push me all you want,"
said Buck.
"I have a test to pass.
And soon."

Thinking It Over

1. What can make you
   want to do something
   you didn't want to do?

2. Do you think
   Buck should have given up
   on the weights?
   Why or why not?

3. Was Lorna smart
   to back off
   when Buck asked her to?
   Why or why not?
   How did Buck come around
   to her way of seeing things?

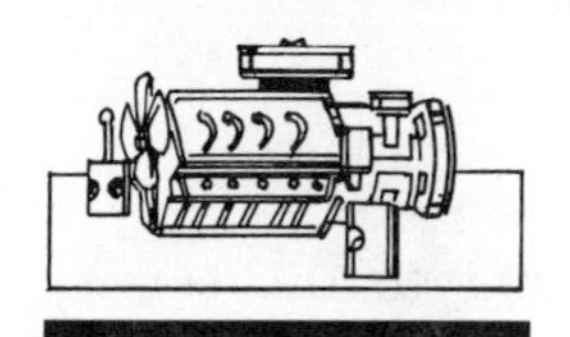

CHAPTER 11

Buck and Lorna
were very busy
the next few weeks.
They worked on the books.
They watched the video.
They listened to a tape.
They checked over a truck
down at Skinner's.

"A new CDL class
starts next Friday,"
Garth told them one day.
"There's nothing to stop you
from going again."

"At this point,
I'll do anything
to help me pass that test,"
said Buck.

So he went to the class
for four more weeks.
He really enjoyed
working on the computer again.

On the last day of class,
Buck took a practice test.
This wasn't the first time.
But it was the first time
he did so well on it.

"Buck, I really believe
you are ready
to go for the CDL test again,"
Candy told him.
"It's next Saturday.
What do you think?"

"I might as well try,"
said Buck.

The next Saturday morning,
Buck headed down
to the fire house

to take the test.
He was the first one in line.
Last time he was there,
so many drivers showed up
that not everyone could get in.
Buck did not want
to wait any longer
to get this thing done.

He took his time
to read each question.
He picked his answers
with great care.
He didn't spend time
on questions he couldn't answer.
But he did mark some
to come back to later.
He also guessed some answers.
He even took a few breaks.
And during the whole time,
he kept his head.
Last time he'd lost his cool.
He wasn't going to let that
happen again.

And then he was finished.
He handed in his paper.
Lorna was waiting outside.
"Did they tell you
if you passed?"
she asked right away.

Buck had a big smile
on his face.
"I didn't wait around
for someone to tell me,"
he answered.
"I know I passed.
And you know why?
Because I had a lot of help."

"You're the one
who did the work,"
said Lorna.

"Sure, I worked for this,"
said Buck.
"But I never could have done it
without you and Candy and Garth
behind me all the way."

"Well, then, go back in
and get your paper,"
said Lorna.
"You'll need it
until your new license comes in."

Buck went back inside,
When he came back out
he waved the paper
high in the air.

He put his other arm
around Lorna.
"You know what, Babe?"
Buck said.
"I've never been more proud
in my whole life.
Never.
Let's go show Garth this paper.
He's not going to hold that job
for me forever."

Thinking It Over

1. What have you done
   that made you
   proud of yourself?
   Why did it make you
   so proud?

2. What makes you proud
   of other people?

3. Does hard work
   always pay off?
   Sometimes?
   Or never?
   Why do you think so?